I0063057

Better Meetings

B. Vincent

Published by RWG Publishing, 2021.

While every precaution has been taken in the preparation of this book, the publisher assumes no responsibility for errors or omissions, or for damages resulting from the use of the information contained herein.

BETTER MEETINGS

First edition. June 17, 2021.

Copyright © 2021 B. Vincent.

Written by B. Vincent.

Also by B. Vincent

Affiliate Marketing
Affiliate Marketing
Affiliate Marketing

Standalone
Affiliate Recruiting
Business Layoffs & Firings
Business and Entrepreneur Guide
Business Remote Workforce
Career Transition
Project Management
Precision Targeting
Professional Development
Strategic Planning
Content Marketing
Imminent List Building
Getting Past GateKeepers
Banner Ads
Bookkeeping

Bridge Pages
Business Acquisition
Business Bogging
Marketing Automation
Better Meetings

Better Meetings

Dave Barry once said, if you had to identify in one word the reason why the human race has not achieved and never will achieve its full potential, that word would be meetings. And Peter Drucker once said, meetings are a symptom of bad organization. The fewer meetings, the better. Now those might sound like pretty pessimistic observations, but it's true. A lot of time gets wasted at meetings. In fact, several studies have shown that poorly optimized meetings are an enormous drain, not just on companies themselves, but even on the economy as a whole. So how do we ensure that your organization doesn't fall victim to this? How can we guarantee that meetings in our organization are effective, efficient, and ultimately a benefit to our businesses rather than a liability. In this course, we're going to show you how to do exactly that.

According to a recent report, the cost of poorly organized meetings in 2019 tallied up to $399 billion in the US and $58 billion in the UK. 44% of workers complained that attending poorly organized meetings negatively impacted the rest of their work. 69% of employees find themselves bored and check their email during meetings and executives admit that they view more than 67% of meetings as failures. These statistics show that better meetings are an increasingly important area that business should focus on. Our course is going to consist of a series of critical discussion points. These are designed to cover this broad topic as thoroughly as possible to encourage growth in these vital areas and to facilitate a real and fruitful discussion within your organization about how you can each improve on this essential characteristic, both at work and in your personal lives in general. Some of these will be pretty lengthy and some will be relatively straightforward and brief. At the very end of this roadmap comes the most important final step; discussion time, do not skip this. This is the most important part of this training. When you finish this course, you need to spend at least an hour or so going over the questions we supply at the end as a group. Whoever's the head honcho in the group should designate a facilitator whose responsibility it is to see that each question is covered and that everyone, time permitting, is able to have their say. Make sure all contributions are valued, all suggestions considered and all opinions respected.

So let's move into the first discussion point, prepare the agenda. The backbone of every successful business meeting is the agenda. As business owners your job is to create an agenda that can vividly outline the goal of your meeting. An agenda is basically a call to action button that should be presented in each meeting you make. Here are ways on how to create your agenda; create it early. Of course you want to avoid last minute preparations. Suppose your meeting is scheduled for Thursday at 3:00 PM, you most certainly won't do it the morning of the actual day. Preparing it in advance gives you more time to think about the pressing issues that need to be resolved immediately. Goals that should be accomplished within certain timeframes and areas that can contribute to the improvement of your business. Identify the needs, as you start creating your agenda you need to answer these important questions; How long should the meeting be? Who are my participants? Where's the location of the meeting? Seek input from your members, if you're planning a team meeting, ask your members if they have any ideas on what to discuss on the agenda. Understand the business in their point of view by allowing them to give reasons on why should a particular topic needs to be discussed. You may be surprised to hear their thoughts on these matters. Gathering their ideas and injecting them into the agenda will contribute to a highly interactive meeting. Categorize your agenda list, as you create the items for your agenda make sure to arrange them by priority. This prevents meetings from getting into overtime. One good tip is to limit your agenda to only five topics. These topics can also be broken down into key points for a more focused discussion.

List your topics as questions, for some businesses it has been their custom to write their agenda items as phrases. However, listing topics as phrases would be too general for your attendees. For example, instead of writing down "Client project management," why not write, "How can we provide more assistance to our clients' projects?" Query converted topics provide more specificity and allow your attendees to become more ready for the meeting. Include additional information, this includes a list of assigned individuals with their corresponding roles and responsibilities during the meeting. For instance, your agenda should include those assigned to distribute the attached documents and who will lead the team discussion. Be clear of your objectives, as an organizer you should make it clear what's the purpose of every meeting you facilitate. These goals are found in your agenda that you've created and distributed to your attendees in advance. As the meeting progresses, you should make it a point that each one of these goals is being answered throughout the discussion. Do not leave the meeting until your needs have been satisfied. Simplify your communication, as someone who has the most knowledge of the topics to be discussed, do not expect that your attendees will have the same level of understanding as you do. You may have certain insight on matters that only a few would understand. This is why you need to develop a plan on how to relay this information in a more simple yet powerful way. For example, instead of using a lot of flowery words or meaningless jargon, why not compose your sentences in a way that's accessible to all? If someone doesn't understand what you're saying, don't lose hope, be patient. Try to reconstruct your phrases so that everyone is on board.

Create a meeting summary, besides the agenda itself, it would be best to distribute a one page summary of the meeting to the attendees. This document lets your employees know what to expect so they can have a better understanding of what the flow will be. Having a meeting summary will help the team to remember the key points and keep track of the things that have already been discussed. The summary should contain the following; decisions that have been made, motions, votes, et cetera, plans for the future, problems and issues and how to resolve them, monthly, quarterly reports of organizational accomplishments. A meeting summary also serves as a track record for those who have been assigned to specific tasks, it could also be used to identify which persons are present during the meeting. This also prevents the group from being gullible to certain rumors amongst coworkers. Organize the physical environment, a good visual environment is conducive to better meetings. Your job is to make sure that everything is arranged properly before the meeting takes place. Normally a meeting should have the following items; speaker stand or table, seats, agendas, microphone, visual aids, video camera, tripod, video conferencing software. When it comes to the arrangement, you need to make sure that the attendees get the most out of the meeting. For example, make sure that everyone has seats and that the chairs are arranged in a way that won't block the view of another person. If taking notes is required, you can provide writing materials. You also need to make sure that your visuals are visible and that your audio is clear. You can use a microphone and pass it on around as the team participates. If your meeting size has become too large that it won't fit in one conference room, then make sure to use a video conference software to stream the meeting in other locations.

Establish a dress code, this might be self-explanatory but when you think about it, your image can affect the impact of your business meeting. Of course we don't want to look as if we're making a fashion statement, but rather having a neat and professional attire enables the team to have visual cohesion. Having a standard dress code provides a sense of belonging, letting your employees feel like they are part of the group. A unified attire also symbolizes that you all are working towards one purpose, reflects the company's goals and visions. The way you dress can give a hint of what kind of company you're working at. Dressing lousy could give a negative connotation to your company. Whatever our dress code is, it's important that we make a positive impression on others on and off our workplace. Cap the number of attendees, startup owners often have the tendency to invite every single employee, especially for small companies. However, having a lot of people involved can affect the effectiveness and the overall vibe of the meeting. In fact, it can add more stress and consume more time to facilitate a large group. This is why it would be best to cap the number of attendees. Having a few people involved means that the meeting can easily be managed, helping the organizer to meet their objectives more easily.

Establish a leader, decision makers are in itself important for a successful meeting. However, what's more important is to determine who should be assigned to take charge in every session. Business owners should establish a clear leader for every meeting. A leader prevents someone from steering the meeting off the rails. A leader also has the ability to hold the floor at all times. Everyone will benefit when a good leader performs his role and upholds it. Be punctual, a lot of movies have definitely misrepresented meetings as something to be less prioritized. In fact, have you noticed that most of the time, the main actor or actress will come in late for an important meeting? This inaccurate portrayal on television just goes to show how most employees have lost their appreciation for such matters. Why is punctuality such an important aspect of meetings? Here are a few reasons; affects public perception. When you're known as someone who's chronically late, your team will most likely see you as someone who is lazy and unprofessional. On the other hand, if you have established a reputation for being punctual, people would perceive you as someone who's well-prepared and values professionalism. Displays leadership, those who arrive on time are more prepared throughout the day, resulting in less stress in the workplace. Someone who arrives a few minutes early in a meeting allows himself to relax, take a deep breath, grab a cup of coffee and take a last look at the agenda before the discussion. Someone who was punctual at work, manifests qualities such as determination, loyalty and professionalism. These traits reflect what a leader should be.

True, being late can seem to be inevitable. However, if you arrived behind on time, make sure to show respect at all times. If you are the team leader, humbly explain your situation and briefly apologize to the team. If you're an employee, make sure to show respect at all times, for example, be as unobtrusive as possible when you enter the room. If a formal presentation is going on, it would be best to wait until there's a break so you can slip in without attracting too much attention. Start with an ice breaker, before you dive into the serious matters why not start off with something to warm up the crowd? Why not start with an ice breaker? Icebreakers are activities that stimulate the mind of the attendees. Asking a simple yet interesting question is enough to spark the interest of an individual. Whatever icebreaker you may choose, remember that its length should depend on the length of the actual meeting. Turn off your gadgets, did your phone ever ring during a meeting? You might be embarrassed as they stare at you and shake their heads. Yes, there's nothing more insulting in a meeting than to be pulling out their gadgets in the middle of a discussion. Not only is it rude, but it also gives a clear signal to everyone, especially your boss that you're not giving your 100%. In fact, simply placing your phone on the table, signifies that you are bored, uninterested or distracted. Keep in mind what's your real purpose for attending that meeting. Before you enter the conference room, switch off your smartphone, tablet or any gadget that wouldn't be needed for the event. However, there will be times that you will really need to have access to your gadgets, such as your smartphone. These instances include dealing with a family emergency or a very urgent phone call from one of your top clients. In these situations, it would be best to explain to the group why you need to keep this on and kindly ask their permission to leave it turned on. Make sure to put it in a vibrate mode to avoid distractions.

Encourage interaction, if you're an employee, there have been times that you might've felt out of place during a meeting. The reason is that it seems that your only job is to listen, listen, and listen. However, it's imperative that every person in the group should feel that their attendance is worthwhile and that their contribution is highly valued. As a facilitator, your job is to encourage participation among the group. How can you spur participation within the group? Consider these practical tips; encourage preparation. A good tip for better participation is to encourage your attendees to prepare their questions in advance. During the meeting, ask them to provide updates or ask questions. A well-prepared inquiry will surely benefit the whole team and will let them feel that they are essential. Involve everyone, for facilitators, your job is to make sure that everyone in attendance should have a share in the discussion. If you have new hires or so-called introverts, why not let them have a say? Giving everyone a chance to express their thoughts means that you value their opinions. Participating also allows them to appreciate the purpose of such meetings. Entertain various questions, when it comes to participating, everyone has a different point of view. Some prefer straightforward questions, while others want to tackle conceptual issues. Knowing this, you should make it a point to approach such questions in a tactful way. In fact, you can initiate thought-provoking topics that can stimulate their minds resulting in a more highly interactive group.

Stay on track, you may find it challenging to stay on topic when there's a lot of people involved, so prepare accordingly. Make sure that you stay in course as the meeting progresses. If you find that the meeting has no sense of direction, or if someone is off the grid politely yet tactfully circle back on the important topics that need to be addressed. Ask the right questions, when talking to your colleagues, you need to ask the right questions in order to get the most out of the discussion. To do that, you need to list down the questions that clearly relate to the current business concerns. If you've asked someone and their answer seems to beat around the bush, skillfully direct them back to give a direct answer that can satisfy your query. Start and finish on time, time is gold. Nobody wants to be there longer than necessary. Make sure that you start and finish the meeting punctually. This prevents your team from having prolonged sessions that will eventually lead to their loss of appreciation for meetings. To be prompt at meetings, create an outline that indicates the topics that really need to be addressed and matters to be discussed. Also allocate time for participation and answering queries. Starting and finishing on time means you value the time of everyone, proving yourself to be an efficient leader to your team.

Don't just hit the road, after your presentation don't just roll out, take this opportunity to know if everybody understood the discussion. You may find out that you may need further explanation for those who had a hard time catching up. Again, be patient, give a generous yet brief amount of time to explain. However, if you really need to leave for an urgent matter, you can inform the group to contact you personally to hear their concerns or that you can answer their queries in the next meeting. Learn from your mistakes, every day is a chance to be better. As the owner, learn how to improve your company's meetings by reviewing your previous presentations. Identify the flaws, find the areas where you need to improve. Another way is to ask for feedback from the attendees and listen to their suggestions. When you find ways for improvement, you enable your company to produce more productive meetings in the future. Spice things up, we don't want our employees to feel that attending meetings are compulsory or that they should be present whether they like it or not. Instead, we want to show that meetings are mediums of fun, interaction and engagement. If you find that your team treats meetings as time-wasters, then maybe it's time to change things up. One way to spice up a meeting is by changing your presentation method. Instead of using the usual format, why not add some animations, graphics, videos, and other visual mediums that can stimulate their interest. It would probably end up like a high school project, but the point is you want to diversify your methods.

Be consistent, success doesn't come from what you do occasionally, it comes from what you do consistently. These words from Marie Forleo can be viewed not only as a personal point of view, but to a business perspective as well. Why is consistency such an important factor in having better meetings? Here are some reasons why; imposes regularity. Having consistent meetings encourages your employees to prepare well for future meetings. It also inspires them to apply regularity in their personal and work schedules. Provide positive emotion, bringing your team together means that various ideas can be brought down to the table. Consistent meetings are mediums for constant brainstorming and collaboration. When you have a regular flow of multifaceted ideas, you create a positive emotion between the employees. It gives them a sense of belonging and a feeling of accomplishment knowing that their thoughts are valued and that their ideas can contribute to the success of the company. Creates company culture, having laid back meetings reduces the stress levels at work. This low stress environment creates excitement, enabling your employees to appreciate meetings even more. Increases productivity, once consistent, short yet highly productive meetings can help synergize project leaders and members allowing the company to save more time and resources. Defines your organization, regular meetings generate valuable project information that can be used to organize the team and distribute tasks effectively.

Consistent meetings also provide more accurate and detailed records, helping the company to save time and money. Regular meetings aren't always the case. There will be times where there's not much to discuss for the week. If that's the case, then ask yourself these questions; Would this particular matter be worthy of a meeting? Is the matter really urgent? Does it really require physical gathering to discuss it? You may find out that a quick email or a five minute phone call would suffice. Reconsidering whether to have a meeting or not will surely save time and resources for you and for the company. Try holding a standup meeting. It has always been the norm to conduct meetings while sitting on comfy ergonomic chairs, however, feeling too cozy while sitting can affect your mood that would most likely result in feeling bored or much worse, feeling sleepy. However, a recent trend has been sweeping the business world when it comes to holding meetings, this is called stand up meetings. From the name itself, these are meetings that are conducted while everyone is standing, but you may be wondering why should everyone be standing? Well, the purpose is simple, feelings of discomfort. If you stand for long periods, it will force everyone to keep meeting short. Having standup meetings provides more efficiency, diversifies the company's culture. Standing up is also beneficial in a health perspective for it burns calories and boosts blood circulation. Stand up meetings in a way raise the awareness of the company's employee health.

Set Mondays as a meeting free day, besides reducing the frequency of meetings, it would also be best to eliminate meetings on certain days. For example, a lot of companies consider Mondays as a meeting free day so employees can return from the weekend feeling fresh and rejuvenated, allowing them to have a great start for the work week ahead. Make use of teleconference calls, there will be times where it's impossible to physically meet for a meeting. A timely example of this is the situation we're facing today, COVID-19. A deadly virus that is now considered a pandemic has been spreading across multiple countries, including the United States. Your area might be under quarantine and has been temporarily locked down. Another simple example is working on a remote business. With these situations, businesses should consider alternatives to continue their meetings while working at home. Fortunately, technology has made it possible for a lot of companies to hold meetings by means of teleconference calls. These softwares allow multiple members to conduct meetings and discuss agendas all in the comfort of their own homes. Here are the top video conferencing softwares that you can use for your business; skype for business, Join me, RingCentral meetings, Google Hangouts, Cisco WebEx, and zoom. When choosing a video conferencing software, you have to look for these key features; auto framing, automatically adjusts to the right angle for proper viewing, live chat, can communicate to the group or one-on-one in real time, speaker tracking, system automatically detects the active speaker and zooms in on that person to clearly see his body movements and gestures, noise cancellation, removes unwanted noise, remote management, be able to access other computers for technical assistance, camera resolution, supports 4k resolution for a better experience, optical zoom, enhances video image quality, mobile optimization, compatible with Android and iOS, content sharing, allows screen-sharing and file transfer.

Provide food at the meeting, you might be thinking, why would I provide food? Our meetings are right after lunch. True, you're not giving out food to feed them. Food relaxes the atmosphere and helps the attendees feel comfortable. Certain food also helps in boosting energy levels resulting in better retention and productivity. Fortunately, there are a lot of catering services out there that can help, you can Google the nearest food and beverage operations to assist you. A caterers package typically includes food preparation, serving and cleaning. This will avoid delays so you can proceed with the real matters. Offering food is not something to be seen as simply frittering money. It's a real solution that can significantly boost your team's morale and the effectiveness of your meetings.

And now it's discussion time, the most important part of this training. Whoever's the head honcho in the group should designate a facilitator whose responsibility it is that each of the questions you see on your screen is covered and that everyone, time permitting, is able to have their say. Make sure all contributions are valued, all suggestions considered and all opinions respected.

Don't miss out!

Visit the website below and you can sign up to receive emails whenever B. Vincent publishes a new book. There's no charge and no obligation.

https://books2read.com/r/B-A-QWUO-HYPPB

BOOKS 2 READ

Connecting independent readers to independent writers.

Also by B. Vincent

Affiliate Marketing
Affiliate Marketing
Affiliate Marketing

Standalone
Affiliate Recruiting
Business Layoffs & Firings
Business and Entrepreneur Guide
Business Remote Workforce
Career Transition
Project Management
Precision Targeting
Professional Development
Strategic Planning
Content Marketing
Imminent List Building
Getting Past GateKeepers
Banner Ads
Bookkeeping

Bridge Pages
Business Acquisition
Business Bogging
Marketing Automation
Better Meetings

About the Publisher

Accepting manuscripts in the most categories. We love to help people get their words available to the world.

Revival Waves of Glory focus is to provide more options to be published. We do traditional paperbacks, hardcovers, audio books and ebooks all over the world. A traditional royalty-based publisher that offers self-publishing options, Revival Waves provides a very author friendly and transparent publishing process, with President Bill Vincent involved in the full process of your book. Send us your manuscript and we will contact you as soon as possible.

Contact: Bill Vincent at rwgpublishing@yahoo.com www.rwgpublishing.com